Reflective Hearts and Minds at Work: Shaping the World's Future through Christian Education

Reflective Devotional Journal for Educators

Kelly Sadlovsky, Ph.D.

outskirts
press

Outskirts Press, Inc.
http://www.outskirtspress.com

Paperback ISBN: 978-1-4787-8373-2

Outskirts Press and the "OP" logo are trademarks belonging to Outskirts Press, Inc.

PRINTED IN THE UNITED STATES OF AMERICA

DEDICATION

This reflective devotional is dedicated to my husband (John), my children (Sam, Jake, and Meagan) and my grandchildren (Isabella and Olivia) who remind me every day of the importance of Christian living. I also dedicate this to my colleagues of Christian educators at the university, and the very dedicated staff team at Pathways to Play Early Learning Center devoted to high quality care for all children. I was fortunate to have a mentor in Christian education long ago, and her light for Jesus seemed to sparkle in her eyes and touched not just the lives of her peers, but the lives of many students. Thank you, Liz O., for your humble service to others and your faith that could move a mountain. I have special appreciation for Louise A., who is now with our Heavenly Father, for caring for a complete stranger in a time of great need as a messenger for God. I do give all praise to God for this effort, and I will continue to follow the path of Christian service to others demonstrated by Christ's love, mercy, and grace for all of us.

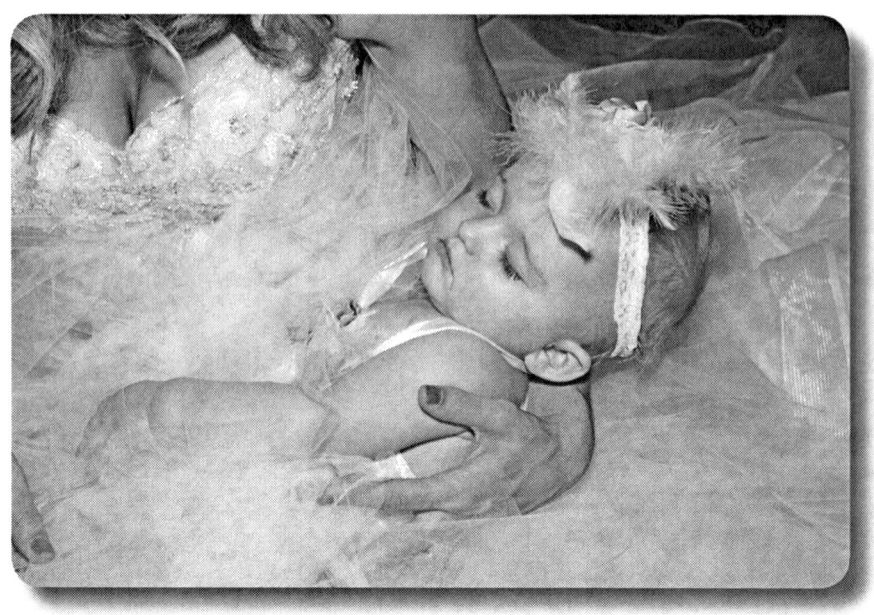

Mark 10: 13-16

People were bringing little children to Jesus for him to place his hands on them, but the disciples rebuked them. When Jesus saw this, he was indignant. He said to them, "Let the little children come to me, and do not hinder them, for the kingdom of God belongs to such as these. Truly I tell you, anyone who will not receive the kingdom of God like a little child will never enter it." And he took the children in his arms, placed his hands on them and blessed them.

TABLE OF CONTENTS

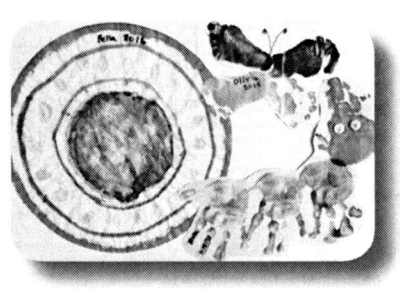

PREFACE

As a Christian educator who has taught in a variety of settings over the past 26 years, I have used self-reflection as my greatest strategy for professional and personal growth. I faced many challenges in environments that were not faith-based, and recognized early on in my practices that I could still reflect God in my teaching and interactions, even in places that I was not free to express my faith "out loud". It was during some of these experiences that I saw the greatest need, and realized that sharing God with others does not require any verbal or written communication, no translators, but instead, when we are serving the Lord as called teachers for any level of learner (children or adults) our actions speak louder than words, our compassion is evident, our respect can be felt, and our sincerity is stamped out in every expression we make without even a single word. We know that believing based on our faith is not something everyone can understand, but the patience and kindness we show others, the selfless acts that serve others first, the demonstrated ability to listen, and the sincere compassion we have for others is what shapes who we are as Christian educators. The field of education today is driven by many different human forces which cause many educators to give-up, their passion seems to burn-out, and the hope that once guided them to this calling is clouded by fear and doubt without support and encouragement needed to continue the journey. My hope is that this reflective devotional helps educators continue no matter where they are in their current practices, adds courage to face challenges that are presented at all stages as an educator, and provides comfort knowing that God has chosen each of us for this particular journey because He always has faith in us even when we do not. May the grace of God be what lightens your load and renews your strength.

This reflective devotional for Christian educators presents 30 weekly devotions to support your current practices and help remind all educators of the differences they make in the lives of every student and the community in whole. Each devotion has a Bible verse (New International Version translation), an application for educators, a reflective writing area, a prayer for the week, and a second reflective writing area to use after making some intentional efforts to use self-reflection to guide improvements in current practices. Reflection is the greatest tool for educators and serves as an on-going self-assessment that should not focus on weaknesses, but strengths, which provides the momentum needed to continually make improvements in educational practices. This devotional does not need to follow in any order, but rather choose the reflections that best meet your needs each week. Use this individually or share your reflections in peer groups to encourage others on your team.

Prayer for Educators:

God, thank you for calling so many wonderful and dedicated teachers to serve students of all ages with kindness, compassion, and grace. Please lift up all educators in your healing embrace reminding them of your love and your strength in times of need. Lord, continue to guide us in all we think, say, and do so that our light for you shines bright for the world to see and provides a much needed example of respect, mercy, and love for all people. Amen

DEVOTION #1   DATE (OPTIONAL):_____

Romans 12:6-7

We have different gifts, according to the grace given to each of us. If your gift is prophesying, then prophesy in accordance with your faith; if it is serving, then serve; if it is teaching, then teach;

REFLECTION: TEACHING IS A SPECIAL CALLING THAT REQUIRES PATIENCE, KINDNESS, AND A WILLINGNESS TO SERVE STUDENTS OF ALL AGES TO THE BEST OF OUR ABILITIES WITH A COMMITMENT TO GOD'S WORD THAT GUIDES US IN ALL WE DO.

Application: As Christian educators, we have a responsibility to demonstrate patience, kindness, and respect in our thoughts, words, and actions. In a society that continues to foster a lack of accountability, encourages the blame to go anywhere else rather than to one's self, and distorts the idea of freedom of speech to encourage disrespect to others with intolerance to diversity, the messages we send to others as Christian educators has never been so important. With the vessel of social media in all of its different forms, the ability to pass on biased information, display negative portraits of religion at any opportunity, and even make false accusations has never been so rapid, and the lack of accountability only feeds the fire. As called servants, we have an opportunity to educate others with knowledge that can end bias, open new perspectives allowing not only tolerance of others, but true acceptance, and to serve as an example to others of what Christ-like leadership truly is.

Practitioner Reflections:

In what ways am I demonstrating this to others as an educator?

_____

_____

_____

_____

_____

_____

What are some of the challenges personally and/or professionally for me?

_____

_____

_____

_____

_____

_____

What are some ways that I could better reflect this in my current practices?

_____

_____

_____

_____

_____

_____

_____

Dear Lord,

Please help me to use the gifts you have provided for me to serve others as an educator, and to remember that teaching is a special calling that should not be taken lightly. Thank you for the opportunities I have to serve, and I ask for your continued guidance in my daily practices that best reflects my Christian faith.

Amen

As I reflect back on this entry, in what ways have I applied this devotion to my practices? In what ways can I further develop this as a Christian educator?

DATE (OPTIONAL): _____

_____
_____
_____
_____
_____
_____
_____
_____

Additional Bible Verses that Apply:

_____
_____
_____
_____
_____
_____

1 Peter 4:10

Each of you should use whatever gift you have received to serve others, as faithful stewards of God's grace in its various forms.

REFLECTION: A TEACHER HAS A RESPONSIBILITY TO SERVE STUDENTS AND SET AN EXAMPLE IN THEIR PRACTICES THAT REFLECTS GOD'S GRACE.

Application: In the absence of faith, there is also an absence of hope. Without hope, fears become reality with no end in sight, which can often lead to isolation and despair. Without faith, grace is not something that we can comprehend, which is evident in those that serve themselves and think that they deserve more based on their actions and are quick to place judgement on others with the same thinking that it is what they deserve. As we represent Christ in our daily interactions with students and our community in whole, we have an opportunity to demonstrate grace by our sincere kindness to others despite the way they treat us, model respect to all, and show compassion to others regardless of the circumstances. Since grace is something that we have been given through God's love, the only way to help others understand it is to display it often so that it can be seen in our actions, heard in our words, and felt through our genuine compassion for others.

Practitioner Reflections:

In what ways am I demonstrating this to others as an educator?

_____

_____

_____

_____

_____

_____

What are some of the challenges personally and/or professionally for me?

_____

_____

_____

_____

_____

_____

_____

_____

What are some ways that I could better reflect this in my current practices?

_____

_____

_____

_____

_____

_____

_____

Dear Lord,

Please help me serve others as a Christian educator to the best of my abilities with examples of humility and grace. I pray for my students, their families, our communities, and our world that is in great need of these things. Help our students take these examples and continue to serve in many capacities that represent your love and mercy for us all.

Amen

As I reflect back on this entry, in what ways have I applied this devotion to my practices? In what ways can I further develop this as a Christian educator?

DATE (OPTIONAL): _____

_____
_____
_____
_____
_____
_____
_____
_____

Additional Bible Verses that Apply:

_____
_____
_____
_____
_____
_____
_____

DEVOTION #3   **DATE (OPTIONAL):**_____

Titus 2:7-8

In everything set them an example by doing what is good. In your teaching show integrity, seriousness and soundness of speech that cannot be condemned, so that those who oppose you may be ashamed because they have nothing bad to say about us.

REFLECTION: THE INTEGRITY OF OUR EDUCATIONAL PROGRAMS IS DEPENDENT ON THE HIGH QUALITY OF LEARNING EXPERIENCES INTENTIONALLY PLANNED AND IMPLEMENTED BY INSTRUCTORS.

Application: Integrity is not based on knowledge, but rather comes from the continuous effort to self-reflect, seek the truth in learning by keeping things in context, and demonstrating ethical practices in all we do. The integrity of our schools is represented by the integrity of our instructors which should reflect our Christian missions and demonstrate a code of ethics that cannot be swayed, but instead stands firm in the midst of any storm. A reputation based on a strong ethical foundation sets us apart from the trends in our society, and provides students with a safe environment to learn and grow with confidence in our programs.

Practitioner Reflections:

In what ways am I demonstrating this to others as an educator?

_____

_____

_____

_____

_____

_____

What are some of the challenges personally and/or professionally for me?

_____

_____

_____

_____

_____

_____

_____

_____

What are some ways that I could better reflect this in my current practices?

_____

_____

_____

_____

_____

_____

_____

_____

Dear Lord,

Please help me to represent integrity in my role as a Christian educator. I recognize the responsibility that comes with serving others, especially in a role of guidance and instruction. Thank you for providing me with countless opportunities to serve others and for the continuous light that guides my path.

Amen

As I reflect back on this entry, in what ways have I applied this devotion to my practices? In what ways can I further develop this as a Christian educator?

DATE (OPTIONAL): _____

_____
_____
_____
_____
_____
_____
_____
_____

Additional Bible Verses that Apply:

_____
_____
_____
_____
_____
_____
_____
_____

Luke 6:40

The student is not above the teacher, but everyone who is fully trained will be like their teacher.

REFLECTION: WHAT WE TEACH IS IMPORTANT, BUT HOW WE TEACH, THE WAY WE TREAT OTHERS, AND THE AWARENESS OF THE IMPACT (POSITIVE OR NEGATIVE) WE CAN HAVE ON STUDENTS SHOULD BE SOMETHING THAT WE CONTINUOUSLY REFLECT UPON IN OUR CURRENT PRACTICES.

Application: As Christian educators, we need to not only be strong in our content knowledge, but consistent in our teaching methods which model respect to students. This can be challenging at times when we are working with students that do not respect us, their peers, or the mission of our programs. This challenge represents an opportunity for us to lead by example demonstrating our ability to be respectful in our communications with students in all capacities. These challenges also lead us to reflect on our teaching methods and continuously find ways to make improvements that best meet the needs of the students in our programs.

Practitioner Reflections:

In what ways am I demonstrating this to others as an educator?

_____

_____

_____

_____

_____

_____

What are some of the challenges personally and/or professionally for me?

_____

_____

_____

_____

_____

_____

_____

_____

What are some ways that I could better reflect this in my current practices?

_____

_____

_____

_____

_____

_____

_____

_____

Dear Lord,

Please give me patience as a Christian educator as I may face adversity with students and families in my program. Help me serve as an example of your mercy and love, despite the actions of others. I pray for the ability to show respect at all times and in all situations.

Amen

As I reflect back on this entry, in what ways have I applied this devotion to my practices? In what ways can I further develop this as a Christian educator?

DATE (OPTIONAL): _____

_____
_____
_____
_____
_____
_____
_____
_____

Additional Bible Verses that Apply:

_____
_____
_____
_____
_____
_____
_____

DEVOTION #5 DATE (OPTIONAL):_____

Romans 2:21

You, then, who teach others, do you not teach yourself? You who preach against stealing, do you steal?

REFLECTION: AS EDUCATORS, IT IS IMPORTANT THAT WE CONTINUE TO BE LIFE-LONG LEARNERS AND EMBRACE NEW KNOWLEDGE THROUGH RESEARCH. WE CAN NOT BE AFRAID OF INFORMATION THAT MAY CHALLENGE OUR OWN PHILOSOPHIES, BUT RATHER EMBRACE THESE IN AN EFFORT TO GAIN NEW PERSPECTIVES THAT HELP US STAY RELEVANT IN OUR FIELD.

Application: For many veteran faculty, the idea of learning new perspectives or intentionally changing teaching methods may lead to defensive feelings stemming from the in-depth level of content knowledge and years of experience in the field. The desire to be a life-long learner open to new ideas and experiences cannot prosper if defensiveness blocks the path. The need to continuously reflect and be willing to embrace new perspectives only makes us stronger as educators and better able to understand those we serve.

Practitioner Reflections:

In what ways am I demonstrating this to others as an educator?

_____

_____

_____

_____

_____

_____

_____

What are some of the challenges personally and/or professionally for me?

_____

_____

_____

_____

_____

_____

_____

_____

What are some ways that I could better reflect this in my current practices?

_____

_____

_____

_____

_____

_____

_____

_____

Dear Lord,

Please help me to continuously seek new information to help me better understand the needs of the students and community I serve. Open my heart and mind to additional perspectives that can often lead to compassion and greater levels of support for those in need.

Amen

As I reflect back on this entry, in what ways have I applied this devotion to my practices? In what ways can I further develop this as a Christian educator?

DATE (OPTIONAL): _____

_____
_____
_____
_____
_____
_____
_____
_____

Additional Bible Verses that Apply:

_____
_____
_____
_____
_____
_____
_____
_____

Psalm 32:8

I will instruct you and teach you in the way you should go; I will counsel you with my loving eye on you.

REFLECTION: DISCIPLINED LEARNING TAKES PRACTICE, AND TO TRULY SERVE OTHERS AS A TEACHER, WE MUST BE AWARE OF STUDENT STRUGGLES AND OFFER SUPPORT WHEN WE CAN TO FOSTER A LOVE FOR LEARNING THAT SEEKS OUT STRENGTHS VERSES WEAKNESSES AND GUIDES OUR INSTRUCTION BASED ON INDIVIDUAL NEEDS.

Application: It takes intentional effort to focus on strengths first, but we want to build on the skills of our students to help them master new skills. When we are helping a student in an area of learning that is challenging, we need to demonstrate patience and kindness that can foster self-confidence leading to a greater desire to learn.

Practitioner Reflections:

In what ways am I demonstrating this to others as an educator?

_____

_____

_____

_____

_____

_____

_____

_____

_____

What are some of the challenges personally and/or professionally for me?

_____

_____

_____

_____

_____

_____

_____

_____

What are some ways that I could better reflect this in my current practices?

_____

_____

_____

_____

_____

_____

_____

_____

Dear Lord,

Please help me encourage the students I serve and foster a love for learning that will stay with them for years to come. For some students that may have had a negative learning experience, this support could change their attitudes towards learning and build their confidence.

Amen

As I reflect back on this entry, in what ways have I applied this devotion to my practices? In what ways can I further develop this as a Christian educator?

DATE (OPTIONAL): _____

_____

_____

_____

_____

_____

_____

_____

Additional Bible Verses that Apply:

_____

_____

_____

_____

_____

_____

_____

_____

James 3:1-2

Not many of you should become teachers, my fellow believers, because you know that we who teach will be judged more strictly. We all stumble in many ways. Anyone who is never at fault in what they say is perfect, able to keep their whole body in check.

REFLECTION: WE ALL MAKE MISTAKES, AND AS TEACHERS, WE HAVE THIS AWESOME OPPORTUNITY TO DEMONSTRATE TO OTHERS HOW WE USE OUR PROBLEM-SOLVING SKILLS AND APPLY COPING SKILLS AS NEEDED.

Application: This example may be one of the most important messages we send to students that associate mistakes with failure. It is not the mistakes that define us, but rather the ability to rise above challenges and continue with determination; this is resiliency.

Practitioner Reflections:

In what ways am I demonstrating this to others as an educator?

_____
_____
_____ _____
_____
_____
_____
_____
_____
_____
_____
_____

What are some of the challenges personally and/or professionally for me?

_____

_____

_____

_____

_____

_____

_____

_____

What are some ways that I could better reflect this in my current practices?

_____

_____

_____

_____

_____

_____

_____

_____

Dear Lord,

Please help me serve as an example to students by displaying resiliency in situations that I can use problem-solving skills, coping mechanisms, and humility to turn a seemingly failure into nothing more than an attempt that I will try again. The success is not in the finished product, but rather should be celebrated with each step of progress we make. Help me to encourage, motivate, and inspire my students.

Amen

As I reflect back on this entry, in what ways have I applied this devotion to my practices? In what ways can I further develop this as a Christian educator?

DATE (OPTIONAL): _____

_____
_____
_____
_____
_____
_____
_____
_____

Additional Bible Verses that Apply:

_____
_____
_____
_____
_____
_____
_____
_____

2 Timothy 3:16

All Scripture is God-breathed and is useful for teaching, rebuking, correcting and training in righteousness,

REFLECTION: AS CHRISTIAN EDUCATORS, WE NEED TO REFLECT OUR CHRISTIAN FAITH IN OUR CURRENT TEACHING PRACTICES AND KNOW THAT THIS IS BASED ON THE MOST CREDIBLE SOURCE WE CAN OFFER, THE BIBLE.

Application: The Bible is often criticized by others and said to be either a good story or just a difference in interpretation, but not factual. As Christian educators, this makes it even more important that we are modeling to others our Christian faith knowing that the Bible guides us in all aspects of our lives. I believe that the Bible is the true word of God, and that the only way for us to reach our heavenly home is to believe in Jesus Christ, our Savior, who died for our sins, not because we deserve that, but through His love for us then and now. God's love does surpass all human understanding, so when many intelligent people in the past, present, and future use science to try and prove the Bible wrong in some way or another, it is important that we as Christians continue to be strong in our faith based on Gods' word and let this be seen through our daily lives as Christian servants. As educators, we need to stand firm on the word of God, let our actions reflect our beliefs, and light the path for others to Christ as we lead the way. I am thankful to have opportunities in my own life to serve the Lord and help others come to know Him as the Holy Spirit has the power to bring light into any heart.

Practitioner Reflections:

In what ways am I demonstrating this to others as an educator?

_____

_____

_____

_____

_____

_____

_____

What are some of the challenges personally and/or professionally for me?

_____

_____

_____

_____

_____

_____

_____

What are some ways that I could better reflect this in my current practices?

_____

_____

_____

_____

_____

_____

Dear Lord,

Please help me continue to grow in my own faith and stay close to God's word. I pray that the Holy Spirit guides me in my interactions with others and that my faith can be seen by all I serve.

Amen

As I reflect back on this entry, in what ways have I applied this devotion to my practices? In what ways can I further develop this as a Christian educator?

DATE (OPTIONAL): _____

_____
_____
_____
_____
_____
_____
_____
_____

Additional Bible Verses that Apply:

_____
_____
_____
_____
_____
_____
_____

DEVOTION #9   DATE (OPTIONAL):_____

Proverbs 22:6

Start children off on the way they should go, and even when they are old they will not turn from it.

REFLECTION: AS CHRISTIAN EDUCATORS, WE WANT TO GUIDE STUDENTS OF ALL AGES IN LEARNING EXPERIENCES THAT FOSTER COMPASSION FOR OTHERS AND CREATE STRONG FOUNDATIONS FOR YEARS TO COME.

Application: As Christian educators, we may or may not be in a setting that we can speak to our students about the Bible, but we can demonstrate compassion and service in our own daily actions with students, families, and community members. These opportunities for us to share our faith with others is part of our mission as Christian disciples. We should continuously seek such opportunities so that God's love can continue to grow in individuals, families, and hopefully globally as we reach out with other Christians to share the good news of salvation through Jesus Christ.

Practitioner Reflections:

In what ways am I demonstrating this to others as an educator?

_____
_____
_____
_____
_____
_____
_____
_____
_____

What are some of the challenges personally and/or professionally for me?

_____

_____

_____

_____

_____

_____

_____

What are some ways that I could better reflect this in my current practices?

_____

_____

_____

_____

_____

_____

_____

Dear Lord,

Please help me demonstrate your love and grace through my daily practices with students, families, and my community. I pray that I may serve to the best of my abilities, and that I provide encouragement for others to do the same.

Amen

As I reflect back on this entry, in what ways have I applied this devotion to my practices? In what ways can I further develop this as a Christian educator?

DATE (OPTIONAL): _____

_____
_____
_____
_____
_____
_____
_____
_____

Additional Bible Verses that Apply:

_____
_____
_____
_____
_____
_____
_____
_____

DEVOTION #10   DATE (OPTIONAL):_____

Deuteronomy 11:18-19

Fix these words of mine in your hearts and minds; tie them as symbols on your hands and bind them on your foreheads. Teach them to your children, talking about them when you sit at home and when you walk along the road, when you lie down and when you get up.

REFLECTION: THE RESPONSIBILITY WE HAVE AS CHRISTIAN EDUCATORS TO CONTINUOUSLY STAY ACTIVE IN OUR OWN FAITH LIFE WITH DAILY DEVOTIONS, FELLOWSHIP OPPORTUNTIES, AND IN PRAYER TO GOD IS IMPORTANT AS THIS HELPS US BEST SERVE OTHERS WITH RENEWED HOPE AND FAITH THAT COMES ONLY FROM OUR LORD.

Application: The opportunity to serve as an educator with Christian beliefs is a divine call of service as we are being tasked to guide students in learning that can have an impact on them for a lifetime. As educators, we are in a position to influence our students of all ages, so it is very important that we continuously self-reflect on any of our own biases so that we do not pass those on to our students, but instead, we offer learning opportunities that are inclusive to all and foster a sense of respect for all people. We need to remind ourselves as educators that our words and actions may be remembered forever in the hearts of our students.

Practitioner Reflections:

In what ways am I demonstrating this to others as an educator?

_____

_____

_____

_____

_____

What are some of the challenges personally and/or professionally for me?

_____

_____

_____

_____

_____

_____

_____

What are some ways that I could better reflect this in my current practices?

_____

_____

_____

_____

_____

_____

_____

Dear Lord,

Please guide me as an educator to stay true to the Bible, and continuously self-reflect on ways I can improve my daily practices to better reflect your love in all I do. Thank you for this responsibility, and I hope to always remain humble as I serve, so that your mercy can be seen clearly by others.

Amen

As I reflect back on this entry, in what ways have I applied this devotion to my practices? In what ways can I further develop this as a Christian educator?

DATE (OPTIONAL): _____

_____
_____
_____
_____
_____
_____
_____
_____

Additional Bible Verses that Apply:

_____
_____
_____
_____
_____
_____
_____
_____

DEVOTION #11   DATE (OPTIONAL):_____

Matthew 5:19

Therefore anyone who sets aside one of the least of these commands and teaches others accordingly will be called least in the kingdom of heaven, but whoever practices and teaches these commands will be called great in the kingdom of heaven.

REFLECTION: WITH SO MANY CONFLICTING RELIGIONS AND LEADERS THAT DO NOT DEMONSTRATE RESPECT TO OTHERS, OUR JOB AS CHRISTIAN EDUCATORS IS CRITICAL. WHILE WE ARE ACCOUNTABLE FOR OUR WORDS, IT IS OUR ACTIONS THAT CAN MAKE A TREMENDOUS IMPACT ON THOSE WE SERVE.

Application: As we plan intentionally as educators to teach students of all ages, we need to be aware of the other messages students may be getting from home, social media, or the community that do not reflect Christian values. With so many opportunities for information to be taken out of context or exploited for negative reasons, educators must stay current in content knowledge, but also stay relevant to the needs of students and aware of other influences that may be leading students astray. We do not want to force our beliefs on anyone, but instead, we want to lead them serving as a positive role model demonstrating integrity and respect.

Practitioner Reflections:

In what ways am I demonstrating this to others as an educator?

_____
_____
_____
_____
_____
_____

What are some of the challenges personally and/or professionally for me?

_____

_____

_____

_____

_____

_____

_____

What are some ways that I could better reflect this in my current practices?

_____

_____

_____

_____

_____

_____

_____

Dear Lord,

Please help me to remain humble in my own service as a Christian educator, and remember that my actions speak louder than my words. I pray that I may continuously reflect on my own interactions with others as we are all sinful by nature. Please continue to light my path and lift me in times of need so that I have renewed strength to serve others.

Amen

As I reflect back on this entry, in what ways have I applied this devotion to my practices? In what ways can I further develop this as a Christian educator?

DATE (OPTIONAL): _____

_____
_____
_____
_____
_____
_____
_____
_____

Additional Bible Verses that Apply:

_____
_____
_____
_____
_____
_____
_____
_____

DEVOTION #12   DATE (OPTIONAL):_____

1 Corinthians 15:58

Therefore, my dear brothers and sisters, stand firm. Let nothing move you. Always give yourselves fully to the work of the Lord, because you know that your labor in the Lord is not in vain.

REFLECTION: CREATING INCLUSIVE ENVIRONMENTS DOES NOT MEAN THAT WE FORGET OUR OWN CHRISTIAN BELIEFS OR VALUES, BUT INSTEAD, IT ALLOWS US TO SEE ADDITIONAL PERSPECTIVES, HELPS US BETTER UNDERSTAND THE STUDENTS WE SERVE, AND PROMOTES A SENSE OF COMMUNITY SENDING A MESSAGE THAT EVERYONE IS VALUED.

Application: Regardless of whether you are currently an educator serving children or adults, creating inclusive environments is important for all students. As educators, we must have a strong foundation to stand upon and the rationale for our beliefs, but we must also set the stage for our students demonstrating our desire to hear new perspectives and show true acceptance for others, rather than just tolerance. Some educators and parents want to shield students from other perspectives, which can lead to isolation, a lack of compassion, and often creates biases which lead to discrimination, hate crimes, and a breakdown of a community. Students will not always be sheltered, and without a platform to learn about diversity in a respectful way, they will not have the coping skills to understand differences, may be fearful of changes, and sadly are not equipped to share their own beliefs with others in a compassionate way.

Practitioner Reflections:

In what ways am I demonstrating this to others as an educator?

_____
_____
_____
_____
_____
_____
_____

What are some of the challenges personally and/or professionally for me?

_____
_____
_____
_____
_____
_____
_____

What are some ways that I could better reflect this in my current practices?

_____
_____
_____
_____
_____
_____

Dear Lord,

Please help me as a Christian educator to create inclusive environments that foster respect and compassion for others. As our students face new challenges daily in their lives, please guide them in their thoughts, words, and actions while providing them with faith, hope, and love known only through your mercy and grace.

Amen

As I reflect back on this entry, in what ways have I applied this devotion to my practices? In what ways can I further develop this as a Christian educator?

DATE (OPTIONAL): _____

_____
_____
_____
_____
_____
_____
_____
_____

Additional Bible Verses that Apply:

_____
_____
_____
_____
_____
_____

1 Peter 3:15

But in your hearts revere Christ as Lord. Always be prepared to give an answer to everyone who asks you to give the reason for the hope that you have. But do this with gentleness and respect.

REFLECTION: DEPENDING UPON THE ENVIRONMENT THAT YOU CURRENTLY TEACH IN, YOU MAY OR MAY NOT BE ABLE TO SPEAK THE WORD OF GOD TO YOUR STUDENTS OR PRAY WITH THEM. STUDENTS NEED TO SEE GOD'S GRACE DEMONSTRATED THROUGH YOUR SERVICE TO OTHERS, AND PRAY THAT THE HOLY SPIRIT TOUCHES THE LIVES OF OUR STUDENTS LEADING THEM TO GOD.

Application: If you are in a Christian environment as an educator, pray often with your students, families, and peers for those you serve, but also, for the many students that may not hear the word of God. When we do have opportunities to share God's word with students or others in our community, please remember to do so with gentleness and respect. For those that do not know God, we do not want to motivate them by fear, but rather with the Gospel and the great news of salvation. As Christians, we know that we need both the Law and the Gospel that God gives us through the Bible, but for those beginning their faith journey, we want to lead them with hope and love, which in turn helps them know God, and only then can they truly understand the need for salvation through Jesus Christ. You would not expect a first time swimmer to do back flips off the diving board, just as we cannot expect others to grasp the amazing gifts from God all at once (except for small children- their ability to believe fully on faith alone speaks to all of us). The best message we can send is one of humility, as none of us deserve salvation on our own, but know that we are only saved by Jesus Christ.

Practitioner Reflections:

In what ways am I demonstrating this to others as an educator?

_____
_____
_____
_____
_____
_____

What are some of the challenges personally and/or professionally for me?

_____
_____
_____
_____
_____
_____

What are some ways that I could better reflect this in my current practices?

_____
_____
_____
_____
_____

Dear Lord,

Please help me guide others with gentleness and respect, which applies to students of all ages. Adult learners are sometimes the most difficult to guide, as they have lost that child-like ability to believe so strongly based on faith alone. Please provide me with the words of encouragement that each student needs individually and continue to watch over all those I serve with your protection and love.

Amen

As I reflect back on this entry, in what ways have I applied this devotion to my practices? In what ways can I further develop this as a Christian educator?

DATE (OPTIONAL): _____

_____
_____
_____
_____
_____
_____
_____

Additional Bible Verses that Apply:

_____
_____
_____
_____
_____
_____
_____

1 Chronicles 25:8

Young and old alike, teacher as well as student, cast lots for their duties.

REFLECTION: TEACHERS ARE CALLED SERVANTS WHETHER THEY ARE IN PUBLIC OR PRIVATE SETTINGS WITH A RESPONSIBILITY TO SERVE THE INDIVIDUAL NEEDS OF STUDENTS TO THE BEST OF THEIR ABILITIES. TEACHERS ARE ALSO HUMAN, SO EACH HAS THEIR OWN UNIQUE CHALLENGES TO FACE AND IMPROVEMENTS TO MAKE.

Application: As Christian educators, we do have a responsibility to the students we serve to guide them in their learning experiences. Educators must remain humble and resist judging others not knowing the individual challenges each person faces. It is important that we try to establish a relationship with students of all ages, so that we can best meet their learning needs with intentional planning and implementation based on authentic assessments.

Practitioner Reflections:

In what ways am I demonstrating this to others as an educator?

_____

_____

_____

_____

_____

_____

_____

_____

_____

What are some of the challenges personally and/or professionally for me?

_____

_____

_____

_____

_____

_____

_____

_____

What are some ways that I could better reflect this in my current practices?

_____

_____

_____

_____

_____

_____

_____

_____

Dear Lord,

Please help me reach out to all students with compassion and respect that fosters a trusting relationship in order to best meet the needs of individual students that I serve. I ask for your guidance with this and in all of my practices so that others can see your bright light through my service.

Amen

As I reflect back on this entry, in what ways have I applied this devotion to my practices? In what ways can I further develop this as a Christian educator?

DATE (OPTIONAL): _____

_____
_____
_____
_____
_____
_____
_____
_____

Additional Bible Verses that Apply:

_____
_____
_____
_____
_____
_____
_____
_____

DEVOTION #15   DATE (OPTIONAL):_____

2 Timothy 1:11

And of this gospel I was appointed a herald and an apostle and a teacher.

REFLECTION: THIS VERSE REMINDS CHRISTIAN EDUCATORS TO NOT ONLY SHARE GOD'S LOVE WITH OUR STUDENTS, WHETHER IT IS IN OUR WORDS, ACTIONS, OR BOTH, BUT ALSO TO SERVE AS A MESSENGER TO OTHERS THAT WILL CONTINUE TO SPREAD THE NEWS OF SALVATION THROUGHOUT THE WORLD.

Application: As educators, it can be easy to get caught up in school politics, family dynamics of our students, or something happening in our own personal lives. We need to start each day in prayer thanking God for another opportunity to serve, and asking for his guidance to help keep us "on track" with our missions and goals. I think it is important to unpack and repack your bag daily, so that you can continuously focus on your priorities and keep your own plate from over flowing.

Practitioner Reflections:

In what ways am I demonstrating this to others as an educator?

_____
_____
_____
_____
_____
_____
_____
_____
_____
_____

What are some of the challenges personally and/or professionally for me?

_____

_____

_____

_____

_____

_____

_____

What are some ways that I could better reflect this in my current practices?

_____

_____

_____

_____

_____

_____

_____

Dear Lord,

Please renew my strength daily through prayer and devotion so that I may stay close to you as I go out into the field to serve others. I pray for the wisdom to know how to pack my bag each day with a focus on my priorities.

Amen

As I reflect back on this entry, in what ways have I applied this devotion to my practices? In what ways can I further develop this as a Christian educator?

DATE (OPTIONAL): _____

_____

_____

_____

_____

_____

_____

_____

_____

Additional Bible Verses that Apply:

_____

_____

_____

_____

_____

_____

_____

_____

Ephesians 4: 11-13

So Christ himself gave the apostles, the prophets, the evangelists, the pastors and teachers, to equip his people for works of service, so that the body of Christ may be built up until we all reach unity in the faith and in the knowledge of the Son of God and become mature, attaining to the whole measure of the fullness of Christ.

REFLECTION: EVEN THOUGH WE HAVE DAYS (SOMETIMES WEEKS) THAT WE DO NOT FEEL FULLY EQUIPPED FOR THE SERVICES TASKED IN FRONT OF US, WE NEED TO REMEMBER THAT IT IS NOT OUR OWN STRENGTH THAT CARRIES US THROUGH, BUT RATHER THE POWER OF GOD WORKING TROUGH US.

Application: Educators often lack the support and encouragement they need from team members and community members to lift them up on difficult days. As Christian educators, we know that God is with us, and that we will be able to accomplish these tasks through his loving support and guidance. We should also look out for others on our team that may need some encouraging words or someone to pray with them to overcome challenges and self-doubt.

Practitioner Reflections:

In what ways am I demonstrating this to others as an educator?

_____

_____

_____

_____

_____

_____

What are some of the challenges personally and/or professionally for me?

_____
_____
_____
_____
_____
_____
_____
_____

What are some ways that I could better reflect this in my current practices?

_____
_____
_____
_____
_____
_____
_____
_____

Dear Lord,

Please provide me with courage and strength to continue my service to students daily. I pray that daily devotions and prayer will help me to stay strong and guide others that may also need encouragement. Thank you for filling my heart with faith, hope, and love that continuously drive my passion for educating others.

Amen

As I reflect back on this entry, in what ways have I applied this devotion to my practices? In what ways can I further develop this as a Christian educator?

DATE (OPTIONAL): _____

_____
_____
_____
_____
_____
_____
_____
_____

Additional Bible Verses that Apply:

_____
_____
_____
_____
_____
_____
_____
_____

DEVOTION #17   **DATE (OPTIONAL):**_____

1 Timothy 2:1-2

I urge, then, first of all, that petitions, prayers, intercession and thanks-giving be made for all people—for kings and all those in authority, that we may live peaceful and quiet lives in all godliness and holiness.

REFLECTION: EDUCATORS ARE LEADERS IN MANY CAPACITIES WHICH PUTS US IN AUTHORITATIVE POSITIONS AT TIMES ON DIFFERENT LEVELS. LEADERS HAVE A RESPONSIBILITY TO SET AN EXAMPLE FOR OTHERS DEMONSTRATING HUMILITY WHICH REQUIRES ON-GOING SELF-REFLECTION TO STAY FOCUSED ON THOSE WE SERVE. LEADERS SHOULD NEVER USE ANY POSITION OF AUTHORITY TO HUMILIATE OR MANIPULATE OTHERS.

Application: For most of us, we can recall a time (either early on in our education or much later) when a teacher did use authority to intimidate students and fear as a motivator. As Christian educators, we want to motivate students of all ages through encouragement, empowering them through learning experiences that boost self-esteem and foster a love for learning which can last a lifetime.

Practitioner Reflections:

In what ways am I demonstrating this to others as an educator?

_____

_____

_____

_____

_____

_____

_____

_____

What are some of the challenges personally and/or professionally for me?

_____

_____

_____

_____

_____

_____

_____

_____

What are some ways that I could better reflect this in my current practices?

_____

_____

_____

_____

_____

_____

_____

_____

Dear Lord,

Please help me to always remain humble in my service, and recognize that the more authority I am given, the greater responsibility I have to those I serve.

Amen

As I reflect back on this entry, in what ways have I applied this devotion to my practices? In what ways can I further develop this as a Christian educator?

DATE (OPTIONAL): _____

_____
_____
_____
_____
_____
_____
_____
_____

Additional Bible Verses that Apply:

_____
_____
_____
_____
_____
_____
_____
_____

James 1:5

If any of you lacks wisdom, you should ask God, who gives generously to all without finding fault, and it will be given to you.

REFLECTION: EDUCATORS NEED TO MODEL LIFE-LONG LEARNING TO STUDENTS TO DEMONSTRATE THAT THERE IS ALWAYS MORE TO LEARN. AS STUDENTS SEE TEACHERS SEEKING NEW KNOWLEDGE AND PERSPECTIVES, IT SETS THE EXAMPLE FOR THEM TO FOLLOW.

Application: Many well-educated teachers for students of all ages get defensive when asked questions they do not know. Rather than seeing this as a short-coming, embrace this excellent moment to demonstrate to students how you react to new learning experiences so that they may be encouraged by you. Educators need to stay relevant to meet the ever-changing needs of students and our communities, which does require effort to seek out learning opportunities that will foster professional growth in current practices.

Practitioner Reflections:

In what ways am I demonstrating this to others as an educator?

_____

_____

_____

_____

_____

_____

_____

_____

_____

What are some of the challenges personally and/or professionally for me?

_____

_____

_____

_____

_____

_____

_____

_____

What are some ways that I could better reflect this in my current practices?

_____

_____

_____

_____

_____

_____

_____

_____

Dear Lord,

Please help me to remember my own need for life-long learning and demonstrate this often to students so that they can start to see their own strengths and areas to improve upon in a positive way.

Amen

As I reflect back on this entry, in what ways have I applied this devotion to my practices? In what ways can I further develop this as a Christian educator?

DATE (OPTIONAL): _____

_____

_____

_____

_____

_____

_____

_____

_____

Additional Bible Verses that Apply:

_____

_____

_____

_____

_____

_____

_____

_____

DEVOTION #19   **DATE (OPTIONAL):**_____

Colossians 3:16

Let the message of Christ dwell among you richly as you teach and admonish one another with all wisdom through psalms, hymns, and songs from the Spirit, singing to God with gratitude in your hearts.

REFLECTION: AS EDUCATORS WE CAN HELP STUDENTS EMBRACE THEIR FAITH JOURNEY THROUGH PRAYER, SONGS, AND DEVOTIONS WITH A SENSE OF GRATITUDE IN ALL WE DO.

Application: There are so many ways that children and adult students can celebrate their faith. Many like to sing praises, others like to attend Bible studies, and some are devoted to missions both close to home and globally. As educators, we want to tap into some of these passions for students and help them find additional resources to support them.

Practitioner Reflections:

In what ways am I demonstrating this to others as an educator?

_____
_____
_____
_____
_____
_____
_____
_____
_____
_____
_____

What are some of the challenges personally and/or professionally for me?

_____

_____

_____

_____

_____

_____

_____

_____

What are some ways that I could better reflect this in my current practices?

_____

_____

_____

_____

_____

_____

_____

_____

Dear Lord,

Please help me guide students with grace and mercy, as you have so willingly done for all people. I am thankful for the many resources that are available to students of all ages, and I pray that I am able to stay current on information and resources to provide support to students.

Amen

As I reflect back on this entry, in what ways have I applied this devotion to my practices? In what ways can I further develop this as a Christian educator?

DATE (OPTIONAL): _____

_____

_____

_____

_____

_____

_____

_____

Additional Bible Verses that Apply:

_____

_____

_____

_____

_____

_____

_____

1 Timothy 4:11

Teach these things and insist that everyone learn them.

REFLECTION: JESUS PROVIDES EDUCATORS WITH THE GREATEST EXAMPLES OF TEACHIING OTHERS WITH PATIENCE, KINDNESS, AND FOREGIVENESS AT ALL TIMES. IT IS NOT ALWAYS EASY TO TEACH STUDENTS SOMETHING THAT THEY DO NOT WANT TO LEARN, SO PART OF THE CHALLENGE IS IN FINDING WAYS TO CONNECT TO STUDENTS, AND BUILD YOUR INTENTIONAL TEACHING APPROACH AROUND THE INTERESTS OF THE STUDENTS YOU SERVE TO CAPTURE THEIR ATTENTION AND MAKE THEM EAGER TO LEARN.

Application: Many educators in the field today, do not have the creative freedom to plan their own curriculum and even decide on implementation strategies for their students. Instead, more and more school districts and early learning corporate programs are telling teachers what to plan, what tools to use, the expectations for student learning, and stifling the natural creativity in educators. Professional educators dedicated to best practices for students of all ages are needed as advocates for high quality learning environments that foster positive learning experiences.

Practitioner Reflections:

In what ways am I demonstrating this to others as an educator?

_____

_____

_____

_____

_____

What are some of the challenges personally and/or professionally for me?

_____

_____

_____

_____

_____

_____

_____

_____

What are some ways that I could better reflect this in my current practices?

_____

_____

_____

_____

_____

_____

_____

_____

Dear Lord,

Thank you for the opportunities in my life to serve others. I pray for all educators that they feel appreciated and valued, and that their ideas are not stifled, but rather are shared collaboratively with team members.

Amen

As I reflect back on this entry, in what ways have I applied this devotion to my practices? In what ways can I further develop this as a Christian educator?

DATE (OPTIONAL): _____

_____

_____

_____

_____

_____

_____

_____

Additional Bible Verses that Apply:

_____

_____

_____

_____

_____

_____

_____

DEVOTION #21   DATE (OPTIONAL):_____

Exodus 4:12

Now go; I will help you speak and will teach you what to say.

REFLECTION: AS CALLED SERVANT EDUCATORS, WE NEED TO TRUST THAT GOD IS WITH US AND WILL PROVIDE THE GUIDANCE WE NEED TO BEST MEET THE NEEDS OF OUR STUDENTS.

Application: Christian educators can often seem like one-man operations, but we should all consider ourselves on the greatest team of all, God's team. God will provide you with the words you need and support you along the way. We are also members of educator teams, so that provides us with additional support from peers who can better understand the challenges we face.

Practitioner Reflections:

In what ways am I demonstrating this to others as an educator?

_____

_____

_____

_____

_____

_____

_____

_____ _____

_____

_____ _____

_____

_____

_____

What are some of the challenges personally and/or professionally for me?

_____

_____

_____

_____

_____

_____

_____

_____

What are some ways that I could better reflect this in my current practices?

_____

_____

_____

_____

_____

_____

_____

_____

Dear Lord,

Thank you for reminding me that I am on your team. It also a good reminder to look at my peers as team members which can add another level of support. Please help me to build on the strengths of others on my team, and to do the same with myself.

Amen

As I reflect back on this entry, in what ways have I applied this devotion to my practices? In what ways can I further develop this as a Christian educator?

DATE (OPTIONAL): _____

_____
_____
_____
_____
_____
_____
_____
_____

Additional Bible Verses that Apply:

_____
_____
_____
_____
_____
_____
_____
_____

Luke 12:12

…for the Holy Spirit will teach you in that very hour what you ought to say.

REFLECTION: AS CHRISTIAN EDUCATORS, WE MAY NOT FEEL THAT WE ARE FULLY EQUIPPED AT TIMES TO TEACH OTHERS, BUT KNOW THAT THE HOLY SPIRIT IS BUSY AT WORK IN THE HEARTS AND MINDS OF OUR STUDENTS.

Application: Educators can often find themselves in the middle of conflicts between students and families or students and unclear policies that are difficult to navigate as a student advocate as well as a dedicated educator. We have to trust that God will guide some of those more challenging discussions that can possibly end in peaceful resolutions. Educators on a team should collaborate often to review the clarity in policies and make improvements that support student success.

Practitioner Reflections:

In what ways am I demonstrating this to others as an educator?

_____

_____

_____

_____

_____

_____

_____

_____

_____

_____

What are some of the challenges personally and/or professionally for me?

_____

_____

_____

_____

_____

_____

_____

What are some ways that I could better reflect this in my current practices?

_____

_____

_____

_____

_____

_____

Dear Lord,

Please guide me in my thoughts, words, and actions so that I may best represent my Christian values at all times. Thank you for the on-going encouragement and support you give me through prayer and devotions. I pray that I can continue to support students with best practices in the field of Education that will leave a lasting impact on them for life. Please guide me in situations where I feel caught in the middle, and really can see the perspectives from both sides as relevant.

Amen

DATE (OPTIONAL): _____

_____

_____

_____

_____

_____

_____

_____

_____

Additional Bible Verses that Apply:

_____

_____

_____

_____

_____

_____

_____

DEVOTION #23   DATE (OPTIONAL): _____

Proverbs 4:13

Hold on to instruction, do not let it go; guard it well, for it is your life.

REFLECTION: THIS VERSE REMINDS US TO HOLD ON TO THE TEACHINGS WE LEARNED IN THE PAST THAT HELPED US TO BUILD A STRONG FOUNDATION, AND LET OUR DAILY LIVES REFLECT THIS OFTEN. AS EDUCATORS, WE WANT TO MODEL THIS TO STUDENTS ENCOURAGING THEM TO ALSO BUILD A STRONG FOUNDATION THAT WILL KEEP THEM BALANCED AS THEY LEARN AND GROW.

Application: One of the common goals for all educators is to stay knowledgeable in the field and relevant to our students. While we are committed to life-long learning, we want to remember the foundation which future learning is built upon. We want to send this message to students so that they too can build additional skills on a solid foundation. With God, all things are possible, and that is a wonderful message for us all.

Practitioner Reflections:

In what ways am I demonstrating this to others as an educator?

_____
_____
_____
_____
_____
_____
_____
_____
_____

What are some of the challenges personally and/or professionally for me?

_____

_____

_____

_____

_____

_____

_____

_____

What are some ways that I could better reflect this in my current practices?

_____

_____

_____

_____

_____

_____

_____

_____

Dear Lord,

Please help me to use the gifts you have provided for me to serve others as an educator, and to remember that teaching is a special calling that should not be taken lightly. Thank you for the opportunities I have to serve, and I ask for your continued guidance in my daily practices that best reflects my Christian faith.

Amen

As I reflect back on this entry, in what ways have I applied this devotion to my practices? In what ways can I further develop this as a Christian educator?

DATE (OPTIONAL): _____

_____
_____
_____
_____
_____
_____
_____
_____

Additional Bible Verses that Apply:

_____
_____
_____
_____
_____
_____
_____
_____

DEVOTION #24   DATE (OPTIONAL):_____

Deuteronomy 32:2-3

Let my teaching fall like rain and my words descend like dew, like showers on new grass, like abundant rain on tender plants. I will proclaim the name of the Lord. Oh, praise the greatness of our God!

REFLECTION: AS EDUCATORS, WE HAVE THE ABILITY TO INFLUENCE OUR STUDENTS IN BOTH POSITIVE OR NEGATIVE WAYS. WHETHER IT IS IN OUR WORDS OR ACTIONS, THE IMPACT WE HAVE ON STUDENTS MAY LAST A LIFETIME. FOR SOME STUDENTS (CHILDREN OR ADULTS), THIS MAY BE THEIR FIRST EXPERIENCE TO HEAR GOD'S WORD OR SEE HIS GRACE THROUGH EACH US AS CHRISTIAN EDUCATORS. THIS IS BOTH HUMBLING AND EXCITING, AS WE HOPE TO LEAD STUDENTS ON A PATH TO SALVATION.

Application: The ability of educators to influence students is great, so we want to focus on ways to make learning experiences both positive and memorable. The verse for this devotion speaks of our teaching as falling rain and includes both "new" and "tender" in regards to the students that we serve marking them as vulnerable to new learning and perspectives. What an awesome opportunity we have to provide a solid foundation for students to thrive upon.

Practitioner Reflections:

In what ways am I demonstrating this to others as an educator?

_____

_____

_____

_____

_____

What are some of the challenges personally and/or professionally for me?

_____

_____

_____

_____

_____

_____

_____

_____

What are some ways that I could better reflect this in my current practices?

_____

_____

_____

_____

_____

_____

_____

_____

Dear Lord,

Please help me gently guide new students recognizing their vulnerability to new information. I pray that the students (of all ages) in my care feel encouraged and valued as part of our classroom community.

Amen

As I reflect back on this entry, in what ways have I applied this devotion to my practices? In what ways can I further develop this as a Christian educator?

DATE (OPTIONAL): _____

_____

_____

_____

_____

_____

_____

_____

_____

Additional Bible Verses that Apply:

_____

_____

_____

_____

_____

_____

_____

_____

DEVOTION #25   DATE (OPTIONAL):_____

Proverbs 16:23-24

The hearts of the wise make their mouths prudent, and their lips promote instruction. Gracious words are a honeycomb, sweet to the soul and healing to the bones.

REFLECTION: AS EDUCATORS, WE MAY BE THE ONLY PERSON THAT OFFERS ENCOURAGEMENT AND PRAISE TO A STUDENT YOUNG OR OLD. A SINCERE SMILE AND KIND WORDS CAN MAKE A HUGE DIFFERENCE IN AN OTHERWISE DIFFICULT DAY FOR SOME STUDENTS.

Application: As Christian educators, we have the opportunity daily to brighten the days of students and peers with a smile and positive attitude. Smiles are often contagious, so how rewarding is it when one smile turns into a classroom full of smiles? Demonstrating to others a heart of gratitude is a great gift to pass along. There are so many reasons why a student may be having a difficult day, and we may not ever truly know, but we can make a positive difference in the lives of all students with genuine care and concern.

Practitioner Reflections:

In what ways am I demonstrating this to others as an educator?

_____
_____
_____
_____
_____
_____
_____
_____
_____

What are some of the challenges personally and/or professionally for me?

_____

_____

_____

_____

_____

_____

_____

What are some ways that I could better reflect this in my current practices?

_____

_____

_____

_____

_____

_____

_____

Dear Lord,

Please help me to spread smiles and encourage others with a positive attitude. There is so much in life to be thankful for, and I am grateful for the opportunities each day to make a difference in the lives of students.

Amen

As I reflect back on this entry, in what ways have I applied this devotion to my practices? In what ways can I further develop this as a Christian educator?

DATE (OPTIONAL): _____

_____

_____

_____

_____

_____

_____

_____

Additional Bible Verses that Apply:

_____

_____

_____

_____

_____

_____

_____

Deuteronomy 31:6

Be strong and courageous. Do not be afraid or terrified because of them, for the Lord your God goes with you; he will never leave you nor forsake you.

REFLECTION: THE WORLD WE LIVE IN TODAY WITH INFORMATION BEING PASSED ON SOCIAL MEDIA VERSES TRUE HUMAN CONVERSATIONS WITH THOSE WE CAN TRUST OFTEN LEADS TO MISCOMMUNICATIONS DUE TO LACK OF CONTEXT AND/OR NEGATIVE EXPLOITATION FOR ATTENTION. WE WANT TO HAVE GENUINE CONVERSATIONS WITH STUDENTS, AND HELP THEM UNDERSTAND THE VALUE OF HUMAN CONNECTIONS.

Application: As educators on any level, we can see the negative influences of social media on both children and adults. While we can appreciate the positive gains for both medical and educational purposes from current technology, we can also see the destruction of healthy conversations between peers, the lack of creativity caused by addictions to screen time, and the disconnection of family members all focused on their own type of media. I praise educators who limit screen time and replace it with live conversations leading to more indepth discussions. The ability to communicate positively with others is important for students of all ages, so this is our opportunity to continue to promote literacy, foster meaningful conversations, and provide live feedback to students in settings where further discussions are encouraged.

Practitioner Reflections:

In what ways am I demonstrating this to others as an educator?

_____

_____

_____

_____

_____

_____

_____

What are some of the challenges personally and/or professionally for me?

_____

_____

_____

_____

_____

_____

What are some ways that I could better reflect this in my current practices?

_____

_____

_____

_____

_____

_____

Dear Lord,

Please help me foster healthy communications with students and peers that promote meaningful conversations. I pray that families have more quality time together and opt to "step back" some each day from the constant connections to social media to form healthier bonds and lasting relationships.

Amen

As I reflect back on this entry, in what ways have I applied this devotion to my practices? In what ways can I further develop this as a Christian educator?

DATE (OPTIONAL): _____

_____
_____
_____
_____
_____
_____
_____
_____

Additional Bible Verses that Apply:

_____
_____
_____
_____
_____
_____

Philippians 4:13

I can do all this through him who gives me strength.

REFLECTION: OUR STRENGTH AS CHRISTIAN EDUCATORS COMES FROM OUR LORD, WHO NOT ONLY LIFTS US UP IN TIMES OF NEED, BUT ALSO CARRIES US ON DAYS WE MAY NOT BE ABLE TO STAND ON OUR OWN. TEACHING REQUIRES A HIGH LEVEL OF DEDICATION, PERSISTENCE, AND PATIENCE FOR OTHERS.

Application: As educators, we all have days that we barely make it through whether it is due to sickness, lack of sleep, family issues, or just the crazy dynamics of the classroom on any given day. We can rest assured that God does provide us with strength when needed and hope when we feel discouraged. Demonstrating coping skills to students is an excellent way to teach them problem-solving skills fostering resiliency that is much needed in life.

Practitioner Reflections:

In what ways am I demonstrating this to others as an educator?

_____

_____

_____

_____

_____

_____

_____

_____

_____

_____

What are some of the challenges personally and/or professionally for me?

_____

_____

_____

_____

_____

_____

_____

_____

What are some ways that I could better reflect this in my current practices?

_____

_____

_____

_____

_____

_____

_____

_____

Dear Lord,

Please help me show resiliency to my students and peers of all ages, as it is one of the greatest characteristics in life with the ability to continue on even when you feel like giving up. I pray for daily strength in my current practices to model coping strategies and problem-solving skills that will support students for years to come.

Amen

As I reflect back on this entry, in what ways have I applied this devotion to my practices? In what ways can I further develop this as a Christian educator?

DATE (OPTIONAL): _____

_____

_____

_____

_____

_____

_____

_____

_____

Additional Bible Verses that Apply:

_____

_____

_____

_____

_____

_____

_____

_____

Matthew 19:14

Jesus said, "Let the little children come to me, and do not hinder them, for the kingdom of heaven belongs to such as these."

REFLECTION: IT IS A GOOD REMINDER FOR ALL EDUCATORS THAT JESUS WANTED THE LITTLE CHILDREN TO COME TO HIM WITH A FAITH THAT NEEDS NO EXPLANATION. AS WE GROW UP INTO ADULTS AND SOME OF US TEACH ADULT LEARNERS, WE CAN REFLECT BACK ON THIS VERSE KNOWING THAT CHILD-LIKE FAITH DOES NOT DEMAND PROOF, BELIEVES FROM THE HEART RATHER THAN THE MIND, AND HOPES AT ALL TIMES.

Application: Educators for all ages of students need to be knowledgeable in their content areas, continuously reflect on current practices, and stay current on research in the field to guide new learning concepts. While academic learning is important, it does not come from the heart, but rather the mind. We should remind students and ourselves that not all things come from the mind which does not have the capacity to fully understand God, but the Holy Spirit can work wonders in our hearts and boost our faith at all times.

Practitioner Reflections:

In what ways am I demonstrating this to others as an educator?

_____

_____

_____

_____

_____

_____

_____

What are some of the challenges personally and/or professionally for me?

_____

_____

_____

_____

_____

_____

_____

_____

What are some ways that I could better reflect this in my current practices?

_____

_____

_____

_____

_____

_____

_____

_____

Dear Lord,

Please help me reflect on my spiritual health often, and grant me the peace of mind knowing that I am not alone in any problem or situation, but that you are right beside me to guide me and carry me if needed. Renew my faith daily with your amazing love and open my eyes to the miracles that happen all around me.

Amen

As I reflect back on this entry, in what ways have I applied this devotion to my practices? In what ways can I further develop this as a Christian educator?

DATE (OPTIONAL): _____

_____

_____

_____

_____

_____

_____

_____

_____

Additional Bible Verses that Apply:

_____

_____

_____

_____

_____

_____

_____

_____

John 13:13

You call me Teacher and Lord, and you are right, because that's what I am.

REFLECTION: JESUS CHRIST SET THE BEST EXAMPLE FOR US AS EDUCATORS IN HIS GENTLE WAY OF MINISTERING TO THOSE WHO FOLLOWED HIM, HUMBLING HIMSELF FOR THE SAKE OF HUMANITY, AND PROVIDED MANY DEMONSTRATIONS OF HIS SERVICE-MINDED LEADERSHIP AS HE GUIDED OTHERS WITH BOTH THE LAW AND GOSPEL TO REACH HIS ULTIMATE SACRIFICE FOR OUR SALVATION.

Application: As Christian educators, we are supposed to be setting an example to our students and others in our lives modeling respect for all people. We are fortunate to have had the best example of all in Jesus, and though we are not perfect in his footsteps, we can make intentional choices in our lives to represent our Christian faith so others can see and possibly follow the light shining out of us from the Holy Spirit to light up darkness in the lives of many students.

Practitioner Reflections:

In what ways am I demonstrating this to others as an educator?

_____
_____
_____
_____
_____
_____
_____
_____

What are some of the challenges personally and/or professionally for me?

_____

_____

_____

_____

_____

_____

_____

_____

What are some ways that I could better reflect this in my current practices?

_____

_____

_____

_____

_____

_____

_____

_____

Dear Lord,

Please help my light shine bright to serve as a beacon for those lost in a storm of troubles, fear, and isolation. I pray for those students that feel alone and scared, but I know the power of the Holy Spirit can lift any heart out of darkness. Thank you for choosing me to serve others with your example of unconditional love for us all.

Amen

As I reflect back on this entry, in what ways have I applied this devotion to my practices? In what ways can I further develop this as a Christian educator?

DATE (OPTIONAL): _____

_____
_____
_____
_____
_____
_____
_____
_____

Additional Bible Verses that Apply:

_____
_____
_____
_____
_____
_____
_____

Proverbs 22:1

A good name is more desirable than great wealth. Respect is better than silver or gold.

REFLECTION: THOSE THAT TEACH SHOULD NOT DO SO TO BECOME RICH, YET THERE ARE MUCH GREATER REWARDS THAN WEALTH FOR CHRISTIAN EDUCATORS. WE WANT TO REPRESENT BOTH INTEGRITY AND RESPECT FOR OUR CURRENT PRACTICES AND THOSE WE SERVE.

Application: If you counted all the many hours of prep work, lesson planning, and intentionally choosing curriculum that best meets the needs of your students, the amount of time and efforts that educators do each day represents the dedication and passion demonstrated by so many teachers. Educators do not always receive praise or recognition for the impact they have on students and society, but yet are rewarded daily as they see the progress of individual students. The field of Education seeks those that are not self-serving, can put the needs of students above their own, and serve as role models to students, peers, and the community. As we guide students in positive ways and foster compassion and respect, we not only make a difference in the life of a student, but it allows us the ability to shape the world towards Christian living. Do not ever take lightly the calling to teach, as the value of what you do surpasses the understanding of most, but fills an educator's heart with hope for a better tomorrow.

Practitioner Reflections:

In what ways am I demonstrating this to others as an educator?

_____

_____

_____

_____

_____

_____

What are some of the challenges personally and/or professionally for me?

_____

_____

_____

_____

_____

_____

What are some ways that I could better reflect this in my current practices?

_____

_____

_____

_____

_____

_____

Dear Lord,

Please help me to stay motivated by things other than material wealth, and continue to offer support to all educators that may not be receiving the encouragement and support they need. May the hearts of educators be filled with faith, hope, and love in abundance; the service they provide in society is priceless.

Amen

As I reflect back on this entry, in what ways have I applied this devotion to my practices? In what ways can I further develop this as a Christian educator?

DATE (OPTIONAL): _____

_____
_____
_____
_____
_____
_____
_____

Additional Bible Verses that Apply:

_____
_____
_____
_____
_____
_____

Information about the Author's Life Experiences and Faith Journey

I felt compelled to write this reflective devotional journal for educators due to the great number of student teachers and educators I work with on a daily basis that are often feeling drained and in need of additional support. I pray that this journal is helpful in recognizing strengths and areas for improvements that can sometimes be difficult to see without reflection. I also want to remind educators in all environments, that the impact they have on students, either positive or negative, can last a lifetime. I am sharing part of my story that demonstrates the profound impact others can have on us, sometimes without even knowing it.

My own journey in Early Childhood Education began over 26 years ago, highly influenced by having my first two children and recognizing the lack of quality care at the time. This was unacceptable to me so I started a family childcare program in my home on an Air Force Base where I could keep my own children and others safe, cared for, and nurtured at all times. Children need a sense of security and to feel loved as basic needs. I am going to share part of my life's story that guided me to where I am today as a child advocate, an educator, and a humble Christian servant.

I am from Texas, and I grew up in a very dysfunctional family that lacked cohesiveness in any way. My father died on Christmas Eve in a motorcycle accident when I was ten, and my mother had already left him at the time. My mother had a pattern from going from one relationship to another, often not taking the safety of my brother or myself into consideration. She had kept me away from my father and grandparents on his side for almost five years with no visitation, and after being reunited with him at nine, I lost him only a year later. I regret not knowing him better, but the memories that I do have are very special to me.

This story is not about failure or challenges, but rather resiliency and a life-long faith journey leading me exactly where I am today. Though I was not brought up in a Christian home, I did have a wonderful elderly neighbor for a short period of time who seemed to know that I was not okay, and she took me to her Christian Vacation Bible School (VBS) which I thought was AMAZING. They had food, games, and everyone was so nice to each other which was not something I was used to. I told her I knew the man hanging on the cross, as he had comforted me many times when I was scared or abandoned. I remember asking what his name was, and that was the first time I knew it was Jesus. His face was not always clear to me when he comforted me, but I knew it was him without a doubt as soon as I saw him at the church. This brought me great comfort, and though I would not go again to church for years to come (we moved again shortly after this experience), I held on tight to Jesus knowing without a doubt that he was holding on tight to me. Through my teenage years, I struggled with my faith, I wondered at times why God let bad things happen, and I had to come to terms with some very real things that had happened in my life. Even when I did not stay close to God, He stayed close to me.

As we bounced around from school to school, house to house, family to family, it was difficult to make trusting bonds with others especially with so many strangers in and out of our living spaces. Unfortunately, alcohol and drugs were also very present, which only made many situations more volatile. Growing up with multiple abusers without the protection of the one parent I had left, I developed a strong sense of protection for those I care for. Though I could not protect myself or my brother at that stage in life, these experiences would lead to an even stronger need for safety and security for those I love.

Going to school in Texas requires proof of housing in each district, and since we were in and out of apartments, an abandoned lake home, or worse, it was difficult to provide the documentation needed to stay at one school for any given time. Between the ages of fourteen and sixteen, my mother started leaving for longer periods of time with no way of contacting her for days or even knowing if she was alive. When it came time to prove my residence to stay at the second high school in less than two years, I did not have the proof I needed, much less a permanent address at all. I had already come to the decision that I would not switch schools again, and I needed more hours to work to support myself. A very discouraging school counselor told me that I was throwing my life away by dropping out and that statistics showed that I would not make it to college or get a decent job. Looking back, it is sad that she made no attempt to find out more about the underlying issues and the fact that I could not prove my place of residence because I did NOT have one.

That was all the "encouragement" I needed at the time, as I seem to be very motivated by those "downers" in life that simply don't care to help, but do like to discourage others. Fully aware of the challenges, I dropped out at the age of 16, immediately took the GED, started at San Antonio College that same semester, and worked 2-3 jobs to make ends meet. I was fortunate to have many friends that let me "camp out" in closets, garages, etc. when I had no place to go. As an adult, I look back thinking I would be terrified for my own children, but truthfully, at the time, I don't think I truly grasped the seriousness of the situation. I was no longer being abused by adults that I could not escape in previous conditions, so I actually thought it was good at the time. My brother joined the Navy, and he channeled his years of adversity into becoming a decorated Navy Seal, who I seldom see, but am very proud of for his amazing accomplishments and refusal to give up.

At eighteen, I got married to one of my very best friends who also had a dysfunctional family at the time, and we sort of took care of each other in our young adulthood. My mother was still in my life from time to time battling both physical and mental illnesses, but as I got older and had more negative experiences with her that caused great safety concerns for my own young children, I eventually put an order of protection in place to set safe boundaries. That is a very difficult thing to do, but my own safety had never been as important to me as the safety of my own children, so the decision was the only one I could make in good faith to keep my children safe from the things that I was not safe from. I continue to pray for my mother, and though I need boundaries to feel safe, this is also a great loss in my life.

My first husband and I decided that we were better off as friends, and he was not quite ready to be a father at the time. Even though we have always remained close friends, the loss of that relationship was huge for me. We were two young survivors raising two adorable children the best we could, and I knew that the decision was in the best interest for all of us. I met my current husband while he was stationed down in Texas, and I was bartending as a single mom so that I could still go to school (studying English with Elementary Education), have daylight hours with the kids, and work late nights to avoid being away from them as much as possible. I had some friends and family that helped me with the kids, but that was a difficult time in my life (I did not really factor in sleep!!). My current husband and I dated long distance when he returned to Minnesota, and I made the decision to move up north in the summer of 1993. Distance provided me additional security which is still a basic need. I had some challenges to work through for the first few years, but I am still here, though I do not handle the winters any better than I did 24 years ago!

Some things I have learned through personal experience, work experience, and teaching a few Family Systems courses include: 1.) Abusive cycles can be stopped by just one person deciding to make that happen. 2.) It is okay to set safe boundaries for yourself and loved ones as needed. 3.) You can love and forgive people, but safety and security may always be an issue that keeps you apart. 4.) It is not the "failures" in our lives that define us, but rather the ability to get back up time and again that shows our true resiliency. 5.) Adversity in life can be painful, yet it is in those most difficult times that we seek God the most. 6.) I am living proof that God does exist, He does protect, He does listen, and He never gives up on us.

I am proud to say that I now have three grown children and two beautiful granddaughters that bring so much joy into my life!! I ended up continuing my education in Minnesota, but changed my major to Child Development for my undergraduate degree to truly understand the developmental stages of children and how to best support healthy growth and development. I taught in a Christian Day School environment for nine years with my children at the same school, and decided to continue on for my Masters in Education with an emphasis in Early Childhood. In 2007, I opened a small child development center serving a majority of high risk families in my own community, and now almost ten years later, we have nearly 180 children and over 45 staff members providing safe, quality care to children.

I went on to get my Ph.D. in Education with an emphasis in Professional Studies and did my research on professional development for early childhood teachers in regards to developmentally appropriate practice. I continue to advocate for high quality care for ALL children. My center supports military families with special scholarships, connects young moms to needed resources, and provides additional support for parents with special needs by providing education to families as well as children to make an impact for the child when not in our care. Health and safety remain the top priorities. This has been a decade-long mission outreach to support children and families in great need which has had many challenges along the way, but God-willing, we are still able to support this community through the many efforts of dedicated educators and my inability to give up.

While I was in graduate school, my husband was called back to active duty Air Force and went on three deployments leaving me back on the home-front with kids in elementary, middle, and high school the first year he was deployed, on top of my full-time job and part-time work as an adjunct at two colleges. I laugh when I hear people planning the "perfect" time to go back to school or start a family…life has a way of making those plans for you! I have now stepped back from the early learning center as an off-site owner (it is in the best of hands!), and I am full-time at a Christian university serving as the Chair for the Department of Graduate Teacher Education and the Coordinator for the MAED- Early Childhood program. I love working with passionate educators that also seek high quality learning experiences for learners of all ages.

My story, I hope, is far from over, but I am so thankful for all of the opportunities God has blessed me with in my life, I am thankful for his protection in my younger years especially, and I am so grateful for the many blessings he has bestowed upon me with family and friends. Being a mother and grandmother does raise my internal "alert system" off the chart at times, and my son's year-long deployment to

Afghanistan, also serving in the Air Force, nearly sent my alert system into some crazy over-drive. I still worry, but realize that I can give my worries to God, as He is always ready for me. God protected my son and brought him home safely, which again leaves me in awe of how much God truly loves us. With God, ALL things are possible.

My prayers go out to all educators struggling to make positive impacts in the lives of students, to all of the children and young adults that need protection, and to all of those caring people that come in and out of our lives leaving a lasting impression allowing us a glimpse of God's love through their kindness and compassion for complete strangers. I will end this part of my story with my favorite Bible verse that brings me comfort:

Psalm 40: 11- Do not withhold your mercy from me, O Lord, may your love and truth always protect me.

Personal Note:

My decision to share some of my personal experiences in this book is based on the intentions to bring relevancy to my applications that are included for each devotion, connect on a different level with readers that have faced similar struggles as my testimonies may offer hope from that perspective, to demonstrate the difference we can make as educators in a positive way being careful not to discourage our students, and to share my faith journey as an example to others of how great God's love is for us. The details I chose to share were difficult for me, and I put much prayer into these considerations, as I have an innate need to protect even those people in my life that have hurt me. In demonstration of Christian living, we can truly forgive others and still love them regardless of what has happened or if those feelings are reciprocated in any way. So often, our sinful human nature wants to return the hurt to others that have hurt us or even worse hurt those that they care about, but that kind of human mentality leads to further division, creates greater barriers, and often can continue for generations fueled by hate instead of love. We see that happening all around us in families, communities, religion, and politics. I have spent over 25 years intentionally stepping back, as even my silence in some ways offers protection. There were many times that Jesus could have used His power to avoid the amount of suffering He knew was coming, but instead He chose to provide us all with an amazing example of showing humility in the face of adversity allowing himself to feel the pain instead of us. While some of those I love, I have lost to death which is part of our humanity, I have also dealt with great loss in order to let God's will be done, and recognize that it is not my place to pass judgement on others. Though I have reached out over the years for some type of reconciliation with those that have hurt me, I understand that only the Holy Spirit can change someone's heart and lead them to repent. I do hope that someday, we will all be reunited in Heaven where there is no pain or loss, only eternal love from a God who witnesses it all. The ability to forgive, show mercy, and demonstrate grace, which none of us deserve, is only possible through God.

Romans 8:14

For those who are led by the Spirit of God are the children of God.

Nana's prayer for Bella and Olivia:

Dear Lord,

Please continue to guide and protect these children and fill them with faith, hope, and love made possible only through your amazing grace. I pray that the light in them shines bright as they lead others to know you and find peace.

Amen

CPSIA information can be obtained
at www.ICGtesting.com
Printed in the USA
FSOW02n2117241216
28803FS